D1540275

"In short, plain-spoken meditations based on her experiences
with suffering and the teachings and practice of yoga and
Buddhism, Betsy Johnson offers a series of much-needed
balms for those suffering from personal and societal wounds—
which, in these times, is all of us. With its emphasis on
breathing deeply and being still, this is a book to read slowly,
mindfully, and with an openness to all life offers."

—Michael N. McGregor, author of *Pure Act:
The Uncommon Life of Robert Lax*

A Hit of Hope

(for when it gets really bad)

Betsy Johnson

LITURGICAL PRESS
Collegeville, Minnesota

www.litpress.org

Cover design by Tara Wiese. Photograph by Betsy Johnson.

1   2   3   4   5   6   7   8   9

Library of Congress Cataloging-in-Publication Data

Names: Johnson, Betsy, 1971– author.

Title: A hit of hope : for when it gets really bad / Betsy Johnson.

Description: Collegeville, Minnesota : Liturgical Press, [2022] | Summary: "In 2018, Betsy Johnson's life went sideways. She knew there were all kinds of things she could do to numb the pain, but she wanted to get better, not worse. In response, she wrote these meditations to bring a hit of hope and help others not only to survive, but to live light"— Provided by publisher.

Identifiers: LCCN 2021045329 (print) | LCCN 2021045330 (ebook) | ISBN 9780814667712 (paperback) | ISBN 9780814667729 (epub) | ISBN 9780814667729 (pdf)

Subjects: LCSH: Conduct of life—Miscellanea. | Hope—Miscellanea. | Meditations.

Classification: LCC BJ1531 .J64 2022 (print) | LCC BJ1531 (ebook) | DDC 170/.44—dc23/eng/20211006

LC record available at https://lccn.loc.gov/2021045329

LC ebook record available at https://lccn.loc.gov/2021045330

"In some ways suffering ceases to be suffering
at the moment it finds a meaning."

Viktor Frankl

Contents

Part Three: Dead Ends

Part Four: My (Tougher) Advice

Part Five: My (Gentler) Advice

Part Six: What You've Done/Are Doing/Will Do

Introduction

This book began in a time when nearly everything in my life was out of my control. I had breast cancer, chemo, radiation, and a divorce I didn't want in the same year. But I believed there was one thing I *could* control: how I would walk through this crucible. I chose to live with hope.

I knew I needed to feed hope the right things, so I sat down one day to do a two-minute meditation I'd found online. Sitting still for that long was all my broken spirit could handle. I pushed play to start the video, and as I settled in, I was told to clear my thoughts. And breathe. About a minute in, the voice started telling me about the benefits of a particular tea. I opened my eyes to see the beautiful woman now holding a steaming cup. Peace with a price tag? Buying something was the last thing I needed at that moment, so I decided to write my own meditations, to use my own voice, which had been slowly silenced, to bring about my healing. Could my words help others? That part I wasn't sure about. Because I knew what I needed to write wasn't going to be "nice." It was going to be gritty. Salty. Real. I had no patience for easy answers at that point.

And sometimes, the swear word was the right word. The perfect way to capture the essence of what I was feeling.

What follows are those first meditations I wrote.

When I was in college, I felt called to go to seminary and become an ordained Presbyterian pastor. Upon arriving, I learned that I was good at asking questions. But I didn't have the faith to sit with the mystery of those questions. I got angry with God—who promised presence, but always felt absent. I imagined myself having to perform a funeral for a child. What could I say about God to parents in that moment? Baffled and disappointed, I quit seminary without being ordained. I went on to preach as a pulpit-supply pastor for about a decade at churches in Illinois that were too small to afford their own pastors. Those congregations didn't mind my questions.

When my then-husband, my children, and I moved back to my home state of Minnesota, I began to explore yoga and Buddhism.

I could actually feel yoga's positive effects flooding me that first time I practiced. I was hooked.

My interest in Buddhism began about a decade ago, when my ex-husband led a study-abroad trip to Japan. After beginning our trip in Tokyo, we traveled to a mountain village. While we were there, early one morning, I walked alone on a small path that snaked up a gentle mountain. At the top, I found an open-air temple. Inside stood three gods. A goddess who was naked on top, one knee softly bent, a half-smile on her lips. Next to her was a massive blob wearing a hat. It was an old tree stump tipped on its side, and the roots reaching up and out made it look like a star. Lastly, a Buddha wearing a hat. A white band was tied under his chin. It felt right to bow, and when I straightened, I whispered, "Oh my." Granite might be dead, but this Buddha looked alive. His eyes—which were nothing but slits in a stone face—took me in, missing nothing. I felt no judgment in them. Only awareness, pure and deep. With a walking stick in one hand and a bowl in the other, it looked as if he had paused here on top of this mountain to talk to the other two gods and catch his breath before continuing on his eternal journey.

Two hours later, we were on a train, rushing down the mountain, and my restless mind was tempted to offer all my adoration to the Buddha back there. As long as I was willing to climb a mountain, he was willing to stand before me, and his message couldn't have been clearer: Be here.

What was so appealing is that I could *see* him. The God I was raised to believe in did not stand in a thousand places the way the Buddha did all over Japan.

With Buddhism, I didn't have to wait for a God who might or might not show up. I didn't have to deal with the wild and unpredictable Spirit. With Buddhism, I was in charge. I had all the control. Or at least I could have all the control, if I could only figure out how to settle my mind, get out of my negative samskaras (patterns), and move myself toward Enlightenment.

But as I went through my cancer treatment and divorce, it seldom worked when I told myself, "If only I could just let these excruciating feelings pass like storm clouds, then I would be free." I could barely breathe sometimes, let alone feel equanimity in my mind.

I failed again and again, and I felt so very alone.

Buddhism never presented me with Calvin's exacting and ever-unpleased God, but it created a different kind of absence. There was no Presence there to be with me. As I sat on my meditation bench, or in the chemo chair, I was alone—in my life and in my heart.

The only way I could think to deal with the bewildering uncertainties of life and Life was to start writing these meditations. As I did so, I continued to swing between Buddhism and Christianity—a tension that I first wrestled with on that trip to Japan. After we'd left the mountain village and returned to our apartment in Tokyo, I sat in a chair and read *Orthodoxy* by G.K. Chesterton. He said that one of the most appealing things about Buddhism was its emphasis on immanence, on being here. He argued that Christianity is different. "Love desires personality; therefore love desires division. It is the instinct of Christianity to be glad that God has broken the universe into little pieces, because they are living pieces."

In Japan—and everywhere else—I wanted a god. Here. In the world. One I could climb a mountain to go visit, one I could touch, or snuggle up beside and be content. One who would let me come back to the world again and again until I got it right.

But the more I thought about it, the more I decided that a cold stone god on a mountain and reincarnation weren't enough for me. Even back then (long before the quarantine), there were already times when life felt endless to me, when I reached a place of such internal aridity, that I was not sure if I could—or wanted to—go on. To have to live again and again suddenly felt like a trial, not a blessing.

That day in Tokyo, I knew something that I continue to forget more often than I'd like: I need a Who. A God who loves me. A God who loves *me*. One who broke the universe into pieces, living pieces—of which I am one among many. Because then I was not alone—I was surrounded by the presences of God. Because then I did not dare to hurt this world, for that would be hurting the divine. Because then I had to slow down and look more closely, since this is my only shot at this thing called life. I had to search in order that I might find—and therefore, I should celebrate the me who never stops seeking the divine in all the places and pieces I can find, who meets the dark with words as I claw at my space in an attempt to get at something bigger.

I offer you these hits of hope. May these words be a reminder to you that no matter how long and dark and hard the night, the Light *always* comes back.

Part One

The Way It Is

Trying to be perfect is a kind of hell

It's okay.
It's okay to be sad. To be angry. To be afraid. To be weary.
It's okay to leave the dishes.
It's okay to let the grass grow.
It's okay to fall down.
It's okay to screw up.
It's okay to say, "I don't know."
"I can't do this alone."
"I've done some bad shit."
"I've hurt the ones I love."
It's okay to cry.
To stare at the wall.
To do too much.
To do nothing at all.
It's okay to say, "Not today."
It's okay to say, "I'll try again tomorrow."
It's okay to feel awkward and strange, weird and broken.
What is not okay?
To let the voices inside have their way.

The ones that want to hurt your tender and bruised self.

You do not have to be perfect.

You cannot be perfect.

You are not perfect.

Trying to be perfect is a kind of hell. It will burn you
again and again.

What a blessing, what a relief it is to just be okay.

To be okay with your fears, your mistakes, and your scars.

To be okay for this breath in. And this breath out.

You are okay. You are okay. You are okay.

Most of us would rather have a root canal

Settle yourself.
Let your shoulders relax away from your ears.
Inhale.
Exhale.
Is your inner life working for you or against you?
Do you hide what is going on inside?
Or do you dare to share your inner life?
Your real, authentic, messy, and maybe terrified inner self?
The one who is longing to be seen and heard?
We take so much time, spend so much effort on our
    outer shell.
Our outer shell has to be perfect.
It has to look perfect,
It has to smell perfect.
And most of all, it has to act perfect.
Or at least *act* as if everything is perfect.
When, in reality, the inner life might be howling.
Or crumbling.
When the inner life might be the last thing you have the
    courage to face.

But the inner life will not go away on its own.

The inner life will not grow quiet on its own.

The inner life will not heal on its own.

You.

You have to sit.

You have to stay.

You have to breathe.

You have to face. What's. There.

That is scary as hell, isn't it?

Most of us would rather have a root canal.

Or do whatever we can think of to numb the pain.

But even when you are wounded, you can also be healing.

Have faith in the work you are doing.

Have faith in the inner work you are doing.

Do what you can to plant any positive seeds along your
rocky path.

Stay.

Breathe.

You do not have to stay dark inside.

You do not have to stay broken inside.

You are good.

You are worthy.

Sit.

Do the inner work.

Heal.

Notice when your flaws are in play

You have flaws.

I have flaws.

There are entire industries that are trying to convince us
    to cover our flaws.

We are taught to hide our flaws.

We are told we should bring a knife to our flaws.

But no matter how long or hard we try, we will never get
    rid of our flaws.

That is not the task.

The task is to notice when our flaws are in play.

Oh, we might say, there you are. I see you.

How you are getting ready to jump into this situation.

How you are about to make things worse.

When that happens, notice.

See your flaws.

But look at them the way a dog looks at the human it loves.

I love you.

You are awesome.

You are awesome.

You are awesome.

Life will give you cliffs . . . and strawberries

Sometimes, life can be lovely. There you are, walking in new morning light.

Sometimes, your life can have everyone around you saying, "It is what it is."

This usually means that your life has turned into that old story, the one with a tiger, chasing you from behind.

You run.

You run and you run and you run as the tiger gets closer and closer.

Finally, you fling yourself off a cliff and grab onto a vine.

There is a tiger above.

And look.

There is a tiger below you as well.

And there you are, clinging to the vine.

It is what it is.

It doesn't stop there.

A tiny mouse crawls out of a tiny hole.

And starts gnawing on your vine.

Tiger above.

Tiger below.

And a mouse, chewing on the vine you cling to.

Lo and behold, you spy something else.

A juicy strawberry growing on the side of the cliff.

With one hand, you pluck it, and it is sweet and
    delicious.

Life will give you tigers, mice, and cliffs.

Life will also offer you strawberries.

Look for the strawberries.

Be the strawberry in someone else's life.

And stay. Please, stay.

And see what happens next.

Part Two

Like/As

This isn't a perfect metaphor

It's easy to let the barbs of life sink deep into your
soft flesh.

It's easy to feel as if you are being dragged out of your
comfort zone while you fight and thrash.

But what if you are being pulled out of the dark and into
the light?

Okay, so obviously, a fish pulled out of the water will
gasp and die.

This isn't a perfect metaphor.

But life often dangles goodness right in front of us.

And we miss it.

Because we are too caught up in what is comfortable.

We are too snagged by the past or the future, the
mistakes or the mishaps.

But, can you grab onto the good times? The things you
did right?

Can you revel in them and tell those stories to anyone
who will listen?

Because it is easy to discount them.

To say whatever you did right wasn't a big deal.

To say the good times won't last.

And they won't.

But, do you ever obsess about the good times?

Are you ever consumed with what you did right?

If you are anything like me, probably not.

So, let's try something new.

Let's grab onto the good and not let go.

Let's hold the good in our minds and hearts, in our
   bodies and spirits.

Let's surface.

Where we can blink and gasp at the beautiful,
   shining light.

Like Don Quixote, know adventure awaits

It's here again. The ordinary. The everyday.
And oh, how it can stretch endlessly. How it can begin
    to suffocate.
It's easy to become restless.
To turn to a phone. To buy something.
A new dog, cat, pig, peacock. A new car.
To seek out a new love.
More. New. Bigger. Better.
Or you can take a deep breath in.
You can let your breath out.
You can be still and grow quiet.
You can try to befriend the ordinary.
Your body is not this or that, then or there.
Your body is here. Now.
Bring your breath into the body.
Bring your mind to your breath.
Do not run. Settle.
The ordinary isn't measured by what you've done or what
    you own.

The ordinary is measured by this breath in, this breath out.

The ordinary is measured by the peace and the healing
you feel as you let go.

You can let the familiar crush your spirit. Or try to escape.

Or you can sit. You can be.

You can try and fill your days with stuff.

Or decide that even in the ordinary, especially in the
ordinary, there are satisfactions and pleasures.

Pay attention to the small and the familiar.

Then you can walk through your day, every day, and like
Don Quixote, know adventure awaits.

Consider the boulder

Hey. You. Good on you, for taking a moment to pause.
Breathe.
Inhale.
Exhale.
Consider the boulder.
A water-rounded stone.
A hunk of broken mountain.
Or a piece of rock pushed up and out of the heaving earth.
Boulders can come barreling at you from out of nowhere.
Boulders can block your way.
Boulders must take whatever weather comes along.
They sit.
In the sun.
In the rain.
And snow that melts and refreezes, encasing them in a
    coat of ice.
Cold.
Lifeless.
Consider the boulder.

Do you have a boulder in your life?

Is something barreling at you?

Is something blocking your way?

Is something big and hard being unearthed inside of you?

In general, boulders are considered too big to move alone.

Can you reach out and ask for help?

Can you sit still and breathe?

Consider the boulder of the mountain.

Consider the boulder of the field.

Grounded.

Of this earth.

Be.

Still.

Breathe.

What if you invited more weeds and wild into your life?

Settle your body.

Take a deep inhale.

Let it go.

The world is very good at telling you who you should be.

How you should be.

You should be strong, handsome, capable, beautiful.

Always be useful.

Always do as you are told.

Stay small.

Fit in.

Be perfect.

Be the rose.

The beautiful precious rose.

Don't get me wrong—roses are beautiful.

And there's nothing like smelling the sweet bloom's
     fragrance on a sunny day.

But being a rose is hard work.

It's exhausting.

What if you tried something new?

What if you tried to invite more weeds and wild into your life?

What if you let go of the perfection and fuzzied up the edges?

What if you commit to growing even in the hard places?

Because weeds know a thing or two about surviving in the harshest conditions.

And not just surviving.

Weeds thrive—in a crack of the sidewalk.

Clinging to the side of a slick and weather-battered mountain.

Weeds know how to grow.

Here.

Now.

Settle your body.

Feel your roots reaching down.

Hold on.

Feel the wild and untamed rise up in your body.

Now reach.

Now grow.

Lift your tendrils.

The light is up there.

Your chance to dance in dead leaves

Maybe there is a day stretching out ahead of you.

Maybe it is filled with worry, uncertainty, too much to do and too little time to do it.

Maybe there is a day behind you.

Maybe it is filled with missteps, pain, regret.

Whatever the case may be, inhale.

Exhale.

Let. It. All. Go.

Maybe it is cold.

Maybe it is dark.

Maybe you are feeling alone—whether you are surrounded by people or not.

Maybe it seems as if everyone else is thriving while you are doing everything you can just to survive.

Maybe you feel trapped.

Maybe you feel broken.

Maybe you don't know how to get even the smallest bit of light back into your life.

Maybe you don't know how to get more air.

How to believe.

How to hope.

If you are facing any of those battles, inhale.

Exhale.

Come back to life.

That might be by saying yes.

Come back to your dreams.

No matter how old, how battered they might be.

Come back to your sense of wonder.

Watch a leaf fall. Watch a bird fly.

This is your story.

This is your chance to sing in the cold castle.

This is your chance to dance in the dead leaves.

You. Are. Here.

Get up. Get going.

This is your chance to claim your life, to make your own magic, to set in motion your own happy ending.

Right now, you are alive.

You are still alive.

Dammit, get up. Get going. Get out there.

This is your chance.

Be as still as a wide-open prairie

There are times when you sit and you know.
You can tell a storm is coming and you are powerless to
     stop it.
Sit.
Breathe.
A storm might be coming, but you can still inhale.
Exhale.
Be as still as a wide-open prairie.
Watch the storm build.
Be as still and wide, as grounded and open as a prairie.
Hear the storm coming.
Be still.
Be wide open.
Like a prairie.
The storm might fizzle before it gets to you.
It might pass to the north or to the south.
Or you might whisper, "It's here" as it hits you with a
     force that turns you into a huddled, trembling mess.
Sit.

Breathe.

Inhale.

Exhale.

No matter what shitstorms hit, imagine a space inside
your heart.

Be as still and wide open as a prairie.

Sit.

Breathe.

The bruise-colored sky will clear.

Consider the acorn

It is the tree's pilgrim.

When it is ready, or when a great wind or storm arises,
the acorn drops and makes its way toward new life.

The acorn might bounce into a tangle of thorns.

The acorn might drop into the mud.

The acorn might get crushed.

The acorn might get buried in the earth before the
snow flies.

Let's be honest: the acorn might have preferred to stay
atop the mighty tall oak.

But fall it must.

And then, the acorn must sit.

Wait.

More storms are sure to come and go.

Some nights, it will be so dark and cold.

Sit.

Wait.

An acorn must fall away from what it knows to move
toward life.

An acorn must sit.

Wait.

And all the while hold onto the life and energy at
its core.

In the quiet of the night, in the light of the day, the
acorn must wait until the time is right.

And then the acorn must let go of its protective shell.

Reaching out.

Grounding down.

Lifting up.

Finding the light.

Welcoming the rain.

New life takes time.

New life takes patience.

New life asks us to sit.

Wait.

Soften.

Marvel at the tiny green shoots that suddenly start
to grow.

Peace—like lasagna—doesn't just happen

Hey.

Inhale.

Exhale.

Center yourself.

Here.

Now.

It's tempting.

To buy into the cookie-cutter life.

That it has to be this way and only this way.

That it has to be absolutely perfect.

That it has to be just like everyone else's life, otherwise, you are a big fat failure.

You know what?

The cookie-cutter life is bullshit.

The idea that there is only one way to live and be happy?

The idea that we can get our lives to match what other people's lives are like?

Again, I call bullshit.

And you know what, I doubt their lives are as perfect as we think they are.

But oh, it can be hard to let go of that kind of life,
    especially around the holidays, or especially
    regarding the idea of one true love to save us from
    everything life has to offer.

Yes, that can happen, and yes, it can be wonderful.

But listen very carefully to me.

The cookie-cutter life, the perfect life is not the only way
    to be happy.

Having it or not having it does not make you a success or
    a failure.

You are you.

You are living your life.

You are awesome and weird, real and strange.

You are you.

Live *your* life.

Not the life that someone else is trying to sell you.

Live your life.

Find your people, your purpose.

Find your way to live, love, shine, fall, and get the fuck
    back up again.

You are you.

And isn't that fucking awesome?

If you have a mountain in your life, put on a sturdy pair of shoes

No matter how strong you are, you cannot push your
    mountain aside.

You cannot hide your mountain under your bed.

You cannot dress it up in Grandma's housecoat.

Well, that might be fun to try, but I doubt you would be
    successful.

Maybe you don't have a mountain and you have no idea
    what I'm talking about.

Or maybe you know exactly what I'm talking about—the
    mountain that is there.

An impenetrable thing you can't get around.

A heavy thing crushing the center of your being.

An exhausting thing you have to scale every single day.

I don't know what your mountain is.

It could be sadness.

Grief.

Not fitting in.

Worrying about what's coming next.

A sense of shame.

A feeling of unworthiness.

Sometimes, it might feel as if your mountain is sitting
    right on top of your heart.

Sometimes, it might feel as if your mountain has thrown
    a rope around your neck, so you have to drag it here,
    there, everywhere.

Inhale.

Exhale.

If you have a mountain in your life, get to know it.

See how it rises out of the plains.

See how it has scrappy trees that grow in the harshest
    conditions, and trails that lead up and down.

If you have a mountain in your life, put on a sturdy pair
    of shoes.

Take the first step.

Up. You. Go.

Do the work to reach the top.

Find the blue lake that reflects the sky.

Then sit.

Still.

Inhale.

Exhale.

You are incredible.

Look at you.

Look at how far you've come.

When you have a mountain in your life, honor it.

Then let it lead you up to where the clouds pass and the
    eagles fly.

Even creatures with wings sometimes scream as they wheel in the bluest sky

There are days.

When you are tired.

And hopeless.

When you can't do the work anymore.

The work of being grateful.

The work of finding the good.

The work of getting out of bed.

The work of believing things will change and get better.

When you hit one of those days, or rather when one of those days hits you, stop.

Breathe.

In.

Out.

Maybe all you can see is bleakness.

Loss.

Maybe you are tired of saying goodbye.

Tired of letting go.

If you are weary, rest.

Let something soft hold you.

Let something soft keep you warm.

If you need, weep.

Let the sobs rise.

Let the sobs pass.

Breathe.

In.

Out.

Even creatures with wings sometimes scream as they
wheel in the bluest sky.

Find a nest.

Tuck your wings around you.

O dear one, be held.

Be safe.

Rest.

A door asks you to live somewhere between

A doorway can be an opening.

You can welcome what is on the other side.

A doorway can be a liminal space.

A threshold between this and that.

A door can be a wilderness experience.

You might be asked to move away from all that you
    have known.

A door can be a transition. A stage of life.

Sometimes, you choose to step through.

Sometimes, you are forced through.

Sometimes, the door behind you remains open.

Sometimes, the door is barred fast.

You cannot open it ever again.

What you have known is gone forever.

Sit.

Breathe.

No matter what, a door asks you to live somewhere
    between.

To live caught between what was and what will be.

That can be confusing.

Disorienting.

Maddening.

Sit.

Breathe.

Hey.

You.

Do not stand there, pounding on a door that has been
bricked in.

You are a bad ass with a big heart.

Turn and walk on.

Into the wild new opening.

Part Three

Dead Ends

Don't give me the pat answer

Hi.

How are you?

Don't give me the pat answer. The easy answer.

I mean it.

How *are* you?

Are you balanced, joyful, rested, and grounded?

Did you just laugh out loud at that list?

Are you exhausted?

Depleted?

Drowning?

Thrashing?

Trying to do one more thing, well, two more things
before bed?

Do you feel like you are headed for a crash-and-burn?

If you are in danger of burning out, let me guess, self-
care is the first thing out the window.

I know.

You have things to take care of. People to take care of.
This must get done!

You deserve care, too.

You deserve compassion and kindness, too.

It might feel self-indulgent for you to stop, take a break, take a bath, do something, anything, to care for your aching heart, body, or mind.

You deserve compassion.

You deserve kindness.

You deserve love.

So stop.

Practice taking one breath.

Inhale.

Exhale.

Now, set an intention to practice taking care of yourself, somehow, every single day.

Settle yourself.

Love yourself.

Be in this moment.

Inhabiting this beautiful body that is longing for your attention and care, your kindness and love.

Inhale.

Exhale.

Grow settled and spacious.

You are incredible.

You are precious.

Take. Care.

The world wants you to hide what is weird

It is easy to decide to bury your real self.

It's what the world wants you to do.

The world wants you to be easy.

Simple.

The world wants you to be perfect.

And incredible.

To be interesting.

To be on your best behavior. All of the time.

The world wants you to hide what is weird. Or strange.
    Or what is oh-so-very human about yourself.

The world wants you to be nice.

And quiet.

To shrink.

To be small enough to fit into a box.

But your real self, your luminous and strange self doesn't
    want to go inside the dark and confining box.

Your real self wants to be free.

Your strange self longs to be revealed.

Your luminous self is just waiting to be shared with all of
    the other incredible and beautiful real selves out there.

Do not bury your real self.

Do you hear me?

Do not bury your luminous self.

You are so very strange.

Please, please keep it that way.

Can you quit trying to make a U-turn?

Settle your sitting bones.

Lift through the crown of your head.

Let your shoulders relax.

Let your mind clear.

Inhale.

Exhale.

How are you looking right now?

Not in the mirror, silly.

But how are you looking at the world right now?

You can see everything that's wrong.

You can hate everyone around you.

You can blame others for everything that is happening
to you.

You can be filled with anger, fear, and dread.

You can sit alone and wonder why no one calls.

Or you can see the gifts that life is giving you.

The butterfly that makes it from one side of the road to
the other.

The man driving the garbage truck who pulls over and
gives your dog a treat.

The old friend who calls out of the blue.

The new friend who hugs you and won't let go.

And if none of those things have happened to you?

Can you be the friend who calls?

Can you be the friend who hugs?

Can you be the stranger who gives directions or offers a treat to a dog with a wagging tail?

If you are contracting, can you expand?

If you are hurting, can you help?

Instead of always looking at the past and wishing you had done things differently, can you quit trying to make a U-turn?

Instead of being afraid, can you be brave?

To life—and all of its ups and downs, its pains and joys, its frustrations and surprises, can you give a soft-hearted, a wholehearted *Yes*?

You can live on autopilot

It is easy to get trapped into looking and thinking only
    backwards.

If only . . .

Why did I . . .

How could I . . .

What I should have said or done was . . .

Sometimes, reliving old patterns can help you survive.

After all, you are here.

You are alive.

But sometimes, those old patterns might be holding
    you back.

You can live on autopilot. Doing what you've always done.
    Getting the same results. Fighting the same battles
    again and again.

Or you can sit.

Notice.

Instead of having the same exact reaction, every single
    time, breathe.

Notice.

Which habits might actually be getting in the way of
helping you thrive?

Which habits might be chains, holding you back?

Let go of that which no longer serves you, comfortable
as it may seem.

Sit.

Breathe.

Do not be afraid to change.

This is it.

This is your chance.

To stop stumbling because you are always looking
backwards.

This is your chance to breathe in. And breathe out.

To show up in a different way.

To walk a new path.

And be grateful to your wise and bold self for every new
step that you take.

Just don't let them drive the bus

Gently move your head from side to side and release as
    much tension as you can that you might be holding
    in your neck and shoulders.

Take a deep breath in.

Let it go.

Now, say hello to all the you's hanging out inside of you.

Don't pretend you don't know who I am talking about.

Maybe it's a wee one who is sure everything is their fault.

Or a young one who never felt smart enough.

The one who got picked last.

The one who hated everything they saw in the mirror.

The one who had to be perfect.

The one who was sure they weren't worth anything.

Every self you have been in the past? See them all.
    Acknowledge them.

Someone once told me we have all these old selves in
    us, riding around life with us in the same bus. That's
    fine, she said. Just don't let them drive the bus.

So, to prevent that from happening, quiet yourself.
    Ground yourself.

And when you are ready, listen to their pain—each and
    every one.

And breathe. And breathe. And breathe.

Then imagine the selves you can't wait to be.

The one who shows up and does the work no one else
    wants to do.

The one who is kind to the stranger, who listens to
    a friend.

The one who decides to do something that scares them
    once a week.

Imagine the self who gets the fuck back up.

The self who doesn't have all their shit together, but who
    doesn't give a shit that that's the case.

The self that is you.

Totally, imperfectly, weirdly, wondrously, and
    beautifully you.

Part Four

My (Tougher) Advice

Have a seat

Have a seat.
Settle your sitting bones.
Bring your mind to your breath.
Let me say that again.
Bring your mind to your breath.
Inhale.
Exhale.
Is your mind already off and running?
Bring it back to your breath.
Feel the breath in your body.
Inhale.
Exhale.
Now, what about those shoulders?
Are they up by your ears?
Can you—for this moment—relax?
Release?
Can you let go of the fear and gripping?
Inhale.
Exhale.

That's it.

Breathe.

Sit.

Let go of the past.

Quit worrying about what might come.

Sit.

Breathe.

Stop being polluted by the things you cannot change.

Believe in yourself, right here, right now.

Be on your side.

You are calm, wise, radiant.

You are a bad ass.

Work to encourage the good in you and in your life.

Let the shit go.

Breathe.

Sit.

Trust.

There is plenty of plenty.

Eyes on your own mat

That person over there is doing better than you.

Did you know that?

Do you feel that?

Let's get real.

There's a chorus out there, and it's singing one refrain: you are not enough.

The voices in that choir?

One might be a parent's voice.

Or old flame's.

And we all know, "you are not enough" is at the heart of almost every single advertisement.

Because you must buy their product to make you look, smell, and do better.

Push.

Primp.

Starve.

Stress.

You are not enough.

Why is it so easy to believe those voices?

Why is it so easy to think that when you look at other people's lives?

In yoga, there's a phrase that sometimes gets used. Eyes on your own mat.

Does the person next to you have their feet behind their head?

Isn't that nice for them.

Eyes on your own mat.

If there is someone pacing around the floor of your brainpan, whispering, "You are not enough," eyes on your own mat.

Mind on your own breath.

That tether, holding you here as you inhale.

Exhale.

You do not have to compete.

Or compare.

Tell the voices to hush.

If they don't, throw some salt on them and tell them to fuck off.

Be here.

Be still.

Be clear.

You are enough.

Decide now to be a bad ass with a big heart

You hold such goodness.

But it can be easy to forget that.

It can be easy to get in our own way.

To stop ourselves from being content.

It can be easy to let our habits put off our happiness.

To let our habits keep us stuck in what is comfortable
    rather than what lights us up inside.

You hold such goodness.

Can you resist the messages telling you otherwise?

We get in our own way. We prevent ourselves from
    being content.

How do we do that?

Our habits.

Our habits allow us to put off our happiness.

Our habits reveal our real priorities and values—and
    they are often not the ones we want to have.

This is the only life we get.

Do you want to live every day in the comfort of
    your habits?

Do you want to be ruled by them, even those that are
 no longer serving you? Or the ones that are causing
 you harm?

Or do you want to throw your arms open wide and try
 out new ways of being?

Can you embrace the uncertainty of possibility and leave
 behind your small and fearful self?

Refuse to squander your chances. You do not know how
 many more you will get.

Decide now to be a bad ass with a big heart.

Strike out on the real and twisting path.

Feel the light on your face, the rain on your head.

Brave the hard conversation.

Greet the stranger.

Listen and smile.

Be bored.

Make art.

Give gifts.

Say yes to that which opens you wide, and no to that
 which leaves you exhausted or ashamed.

Refuse to stay safe inside your walls—physical or mental.

Walk into the wild through the open door.

Begin again and fail better

May your love and joy ripen daily.

May you praise as often as you can and find fault as little as you can.

May you care more about being happy than being right.

May you learn how to let go of "should have been" and open to what is being given.

When times are good, may you be grateful and know that nothing lasts.

When times are tough, may you laugh and know that nothing lasts.

When times are good, may you kiss, and love, and celebrate.

When times get tough, may you perform small acts of mending and expect positive outcomes.

When times get really tough, may you, as the Buddha and Beckett say, begin again and fail better.

Remember, love is a decision. You have to choose it again and again.

May you pick your verbs wisely—love, connect, welcome, care, endure, grow, savor.

May you love fiercely, because this all ends.

Because you only get this one life.

Unless you believe in reincarnation.

But even then, you want to live and love well, because
  otherwise you will come back as a chair.

Or a platypus, and be very confused about your identity
  your entire life.

May this be the day that leads you to happiness and joy.

May you remember that with any love story, it's what you
  put into it that brings about the happily ever after.

May blessing upon blessing fall upon you now
  and forever.

Cherish your scars

We all have scars.

From a bike and a sidewalk.

From a knife and a potato.

But if you are anything like me, you might feel
     differently about one scar than you do about another.

Maybe you are proud of one, because it reminds you of
     how hard you fought, how well you played.

Maybe you are ashamed of another, because it brings up
     nothing but suffering, pain, and sorrow.

We all have scars.

Places where we have been wounded.

Outside and in.

Sit.

Breathe.

What matters is how we think about our scars, how we
     talk about them.

When we consider our scars, we can say, "I have been
     wounded. See? Here's the proof."

Sit.

Breathe.

When we consider our scars, we can say, "I was wounded, and I survived."

Sit.

Breathe.

When we consider our scars, we can say, "And now I'm going to carry these scars with me as reminders— reminders that I can be hurt."

Or, "My scars are reminders that I can heal, reminders that I am a bad-ass warrior who is fekkin' fierce. Who gets up again, and again, and again."

Take this chance to let go of all that has happened.

Let go of all that may or may not come.

Cherish your scars.

Cherish your fierce spirit.

Rise and live.

Stoke your inner fire

Everyone's story contains love and mistakes, pride and
kindness, abundance and emptiness, strength and
weakness.

In the midst of these changing tides in your own story,
stand strong.

It's okay to feel the fear in your belly.

But stand. Stay. Meet the fear and uncertainty with
strength.

Face this moment with steadiness. Hold.

Stoke your inner fire.

Gaze steadily at what stands before you and face this
trouble with a fierceness that has you rooting down
and standing tall.

Quiet the voices telling you you can't.

Listen to the ones telling you you can.

Fight for yourself.

Deal with this.

Seek clarity, not certainty.

Be curious, not controlling.

Foster courage. Let go of clinging.

Rise out of your weaknesses and make space for you to
flourish.

Feel the strength and power deep inside your body. You
have what it takes.

It's easy to focus on when and then. "When this happens,
then . . ."

But This. Is. It. This is your life. Inhale. Exhale.

Meet it with your bold self.

Remember the wondrous space

When it hurts, hold on to your center.

When it's hard, hold on to your center.

When you are caught up in things you can't control, hold on to your center.

When you find yourself returning to a pattern that doesn't serve you, return to your center.

When you want to give up, return to your center.

When you don't know where to find the strength to go on, return to your center.

When it's too much, return to your center.

When there's not enough money, help, food, support, kindness, attention, whatever, return to your center.

When it sucks, return to your center.

Maybe cry.

Maybe scream.

Maybe sit with the desolation and hopelessness.

But then remember your center.

Remember that wondrous space inside of you.

The one that is filled with more strength than you can imagine.

The one that surprises you with all of the ways it helps
    you to survive.

Remember the wondrous space.

Return to your center.

Hold on to your center.

And breathe.

In. Out.

In. And out.

May you be free from fear.

May you be safe from harm.

May the light inside shine.

Board by board, nail by nail

It isn't surprising.

We don't have to wait days or even weeks for something anymore.

We can one-click and get it the very next day.

We don't have to plant the seeds, water the seeds, weed the garden, and wait for food to be in season.

We can drive to the grocery store and have strawberries whenever we want.

We don't have to cut down the logs, fit them one on top of one another, and build an entire cabin with our bare hands.

We watch tv shows where an entire house is torn apart and rebuilt in a week.

But when our lives get torn apart—by whatever it is—it takes time to rebuild.

And it takes even more time if we want to rebuild things right.

First, we have to do the work to tear away our outer shells. We have to be bare. So we can see all of the damage.

Oh, isn't it tempting just to slap some nice new outer shell on as quickly as possible?

But the rot, the things eating us from the inside out, all of that is still there.

And if we just cover it up, it will grow, spread, making things weaker and more vulnerable to life's storms.

Okay, fine. The damage is there. Let's hack away at the rotten parts, right?

But that can cause more damage and harm.

So, can we look at what is, can we see the parts that need our attention, can we get to work with intention and finesse, and piece by piece, remove the damaged parts?

And let's not blame the damaged parts. They are already broken.

We simply say, "This needs to be replaced, to bring steadiness, wholeness."

And speaking of whole, if we work to remove the damage, there will be holes.

We might want to shove them full of whatever junk is at hand.

But can we take the time to find the best materials?

Can we rebuild with care?

And rebuilding with care means it is going to take time.

It is going to take skill.

It is going to take the support of friends and family.

It means showing up at the work site every single day— rain or shine—and doing the work.

Board by board.

Nail by nail.

Until one day, what stands before you is strong, stable, and beautiful.

A space you can't wait to settle into, where you feel comfortable, safe, whole.

Dammit, this matters. Trust me.

Settle yourself.
Bring your attention to your breath.
Bring your breath in to your body.
Inhale.
Exhale.
Some days you feel healthy and strong.
And oh my, aren't those good days?
Some days you don't.
You might hurt—inside or out.
You might feel old.
You might feel worn down, worn out.
Maybe you managed to get enough sleep, but you are
    still tired.
Maybe you couldn't sleep at all, and you are so very tired.
You are sure others are happier, healthier, smarter,
    wealthier.
You are sure it's just you.
Struggling.
Inhale.

Exhale.

Bring your attention to your breath.

Bring your breath into your body.

I've learned something recently.

Whatever it is, embrace the state you are in.

Hear me out.

Be okay with you—no matter what state you are in.

Whether you are the weight you want to be or not.

Whether you are in the relationship you want to be in or not.

Whether you have the job, house, dog, kids, car you want or not.

Can you love you?

Can you find the courage, the grit, the strength, the fierceness to love you—no matter what?

Because that's the thing.

Do you hear me?

That's the thing.

You love you.

You honor you.

You serve you.

Dammit, this matters.

Trust me.

You—please—find the beauty in you.

Do not ruin the good with "what if"

So, has this ever happened to you?

Life has been going along, dealing you blow after blow, and you've managed, through grit or grace or a combination of the two, to survive it all.

Aren't you a bad ass?

Aren't you strong?

And you get so used to this—to putting your head down and pushing through the hard stuff—that it seems like that is what life is.

But then, things ease.

Life lets up.

And not only that, but something good suddenly makes an appearance in your story.

Something exciting or breath taking.

And if you can welcome that with open arms, well, bravo you.

But when something good appears in your life, you might be afraid.

Terrified, actually.

How will I get hurt?

When will it all go to hell?

If you have been hurt, if you have been so caught up in the struggle, if you look at your life and the lives of so many other people around you, it can be easy to think that we need to brace ourselves every moment of every day, because sometime soon the shit is sure to hit the woodchopper.

Inhale.

Exhale.

Life can be hard.

Life can be beautiful.

There is pain, love, sorrow, joy.

There is despair.

There is hope.

You never know what is coming.

And you can expect the worst.

You can brace yourself for the worst.

Because then you can protect your very tender heart, right?

You never know what is coming.

Tempting as it is to be afraid and contract, the brave choice is to be vulnerable.

Do not ruin the good with worry.

Do not ruin the good with what if.

Be vulnerable.

Stand with your heart wide open.

Come what may.

There is no magic wand

Here is your life.

Here is your day.

Here is this minute, this breath, this heartbeat.

You might encounter the ordinary today—a line at the bank.

A meeting at work.

You might be waiting today—for a phone call with the results.

For the brambles inside to quit tearing you in all of your tender places.

You might be wondering today—what's the point?

How much longer can I bear this?

You might be hurting today—in body, mind, or spirit.

There is no magic wand.

There is only this breath in.

This breath out.

There is only this moment.

Breathe in.

Breathe out.

We can approach life with striving and force, with anxiety and despair.

Harder! Faster! More! Be afraid! Give up!

But is that really who and how you want to be?

What if you nurture a sense of abundance?

You have enough. You are enough.

Dwell on your goodness, your gifts.

Celebrate the strange that draws the eye.

Feed your capacity for hopefulness, your tendency for gratitude.

Let go of grasping, forcing, controlling.

Be a part of the bigger Story.

The Common Good.

Let go of whatever is getting in the way of that.

Choose here and now—will you decay? Or will you grow?

Part Five

My (Gentler)
Advice

You don't have to do another damn thing

Hey.

You.

Stop. Sit.

Rest. Breathe.

In. Out.

Those voices telling you you can't sit?

Those voices telling you you can't rest?

Those voices telling you you have to do more?

And more?

I've heard them too.

What did you do today?

What did you do this weekend?

What do you do, what do you do, what do you do?

Those voices are all around us.

We can listen to them.

Or we can listen to our bodies.

Our spirits that are crying out:

Hey.

You.

Stop. Sit.

Rest. Breathe.

In. Out.

You are enough.

You have done enough.

You are worthy.

You don't have to do another damn thing.

You.

You are enough.

Sit. Breathe.

In. Out.

Rest. Replenish. Relax.

It's easy to get lost in the loud world.

It's tempting to think fast is always best.

Seek the quiet.

Embrace the slow.

Sit in silence.

Stay.

Stay.

Stay.

Or you can let go of the things that weigh you down

Feel your sitting bones ground.
Feel the crown of your head lifting.
Breathe in.
Breathe out.
Let your shoulders release away from your ears.
Let your jaw relax.
When it gets difficult, imagine you are traveling.
You have a long journey ahead.
You can pack everything you own, because who knows
    what is coming.
Who knows what you might need.
You can load yourself down.
That is one way to travel.
But then you have to lug that weight, everywhere you go.
You have to struggle to carry the load.
Or you can let go of the things that weigh you down.
Like fear.
Or your sense of control.

Life will happen.

Things will happen.

You do not know what is coming.

Travel lightly.

Instead of preparing for every worst-case scenario,
   instead of waiting for life to change or for the good
   to come again, can you imagine right here and right
   now that you are on an adventure—and embrace all
   of the ups and downs, thrills and spills?

Can you imagine that every step you take is going to
   bring you somewhere new?

Can you cross this bridge—and the next one?

It's easy to focus on arriving. When will I get there?
   When will this be over?

It's far more interesting to live each day—even the hard
   ones—with a sense of lightness and wonder.

You never know who you will meet.

You never know what is just around that curve in
   your path.

Encourage what is good

Settle yourself into a comfortable position.
Relax your jaw.
You are centered.
Your body is not in the past.
Your body is not in the future.
Bring your mind to your breath.
Bring your breath into your body.
You are centered.
Do not be in that moment, whatever it may be.
Be in *this* moment.
You are centered.
It doesn't matter what you think you did.
It doesn't matter what mistakes you made.
Work to encourage what is good.
Gently, let go of what is not.
Sit. Still.
Follow your breath.
Connect to your heart.
Some day, this, too, will be a memory.

You can freak out.

Or you can settle in.

To keep going, be *in* and *with* before going *through*.

You are not the victim.

You have power.

Commit to the things you can change.

Choose to turn fear into abundance.

Life's lessons never end.

Quiet yourself and listen.

What thoughts have turned into knives?

If you wouldn't say them to someone you love, do not say
them to yourself.

Refuse to be in an adversarial relationship with yourself.

Rather, open to what is.

Be still. Behold. Embrace. Be bold in your fight.

Quit turning to the things that don't work.

Move away from numbness.

Seek wonder.

Do not give up or give in.

Practice over and over to get to a better self.

Let yes guide you to the next living thing.

Perhaps, you could consider living the gentler verbs

Inhale.
Exhale.
Modern life wants you to do.
Make.
Push.
Succeed.
Surpass.
Force.
Climb.
Conquer.
Hide.
Conform.
Cower.
Pretend.
Bury.
And if those verbs are making you happy, then by all
means, keep living them.

If those verbs are making you unhappy, perhaps you could
  consider living the quieter verbs, the gentler ones.

Sit.

Inhale.

Exhale.

Soften.

Yield.

Open.

Settle.

Ground.

Share.

Reveal.

Listen.

Care.

Offer.

Connect.

Love.

Nourish.

Grow.

Glow.

A practice of endurance

Are you tired of trying to hold it all together?

Are you tired of trying to control what cannot be
controlled?

Breathe in.

Breathe out.

Things break.

Life goes sideways.

Inhale.

Exhale.

Sometimes, there isn't a damn thing you can do about it,
to make it go away, to make it okay.

Breathe in.

Breathe out.

Sometimes, the only thing you can do is to try and right-
size this, make it more manageable.

Sometimes, the only thing you can do is to endure.

And when you are given a practice of endurance, let's be
honest. It's a bitch.

But one good thing is that when the goal is endurance,
    you are not fighting to become something or earn a
    gold star.

To endure is to sit in a chair.

To endure is to take a drink of fresh water.

To endure is to breathe in.

Breathe out.

Simple stuff endures the best.

Rocks endure.

Friends endure.

You. Will. Endure.

You will endure as you walk through this dark.

You will endure tomorrow. And the next day and
    the next.

You will endure until this begins to fade into memory.

And then you will not be who you once were.

You will be stronger. Braver. You will have battle scars
    that you can show off to anyone and everyone.

But until then, no matter what happens, remember, there
    is always time for a new story to take hold. Always.

And if something is big, give it time

Life sometimes pushes you to your edge.
Sit.
Breathe.
Life sometimes pulls you under.
Sit.
Breathe.
Life sometimes stomps on you and leaves you feeling
   crushed.
Sit.
Breathe.
You can get even busier, to ignore the pain.
Sit.
Breathe.
You can do nothing, to avoid more future pain.
Sit.
Breathe.
Or, when there is something that hurts you, when there
   is something to grieve, you can grieve.
Sit.

Breathe.

And if it is something big, give it time.

Sit with it.

Breathe through it.

You'll know. You'll know when you can let go.

Sit.

Breathe.

Be.

Still.

You will make it through this.

You will make it through this.

You will make it through this.

And if you can't live with the uncertainty

Alright, folks. Strap on your thinking caps, because here we go.

According to a variety of somewhat credible websites, a bird's wishbone is technically known as the *furcula*, which is made up of two fused clavicles.

And we got the tradition of snapping wishbones from the Etruscans, an ancient Italian civilization, who loved their chickens.

Apparently, they believed that the birds were oracles and could divine the future.

They even turned the fowl into walking Ouija boards with a bizarre ritual called alectryomancy, which basically translates as "rooster divination."

Sounds crazy, doesn't it?

Not really.

Because when it sucks, when we can barely breathe or hold on one more second, we want to know what's coming next.

We are so damn tired of living with the uncertainty, that we want something, anything, even a rooster, to tell us something good is on the way.

We want to know that this death of everything we once knew and held dear is opening the way for something new. Something better.

And so, whether we are doing rooster divination, or whispering our deepest wishes to a bone we break, we want to believe that, *Congratulations! A new life starts tomorrow!*

Inhale.

Exhale.

Again.

Inhale.

Exhale.

The things outside of you might get better.

And they might not.

Inhale.

Exhale.

When it gets hard, and when you are uncertain, breathe.

Do not doubt yourself.

Be kind to yourself and others.

Inhale.

Exhale.

Live with the uncertainty.

Inhale.

Exhale.

And if you can't live with the uncertainty, if you can't
   bear it, then by all means, go for the rooster
   divination, the tarot cards, the Magic 8 Ball.

Do whatever it takes to survive.

Inhale.

Exhale.

Hold on.

A new beginning is on its way.

Remember, pretty flowers come from shit

You probably know your shortcomings. Perhaps you
  recite them daily, hourly. You know the ways you fail.
  The ways you hurt—yourself and others. The ways
  you could and should do better.

You can choose to pick up those thoughts and let them
  cut you again and again.

You can pick at your flaws like scabs, keeping them fresh
  and raw.

You can ignore them, until they fester.

You can blame others. It must be someone else's fault.

You can get lost in the tangle of "If only," or "No one
  else." You can get lost in the thorns of "Always" and
  "Never."

You can make your faults epic.

Or you can realize you did the best you could. Now that
  you know better, you can do better.

You can see your scars and know that each one of them
  represents a battle you have survived.

You can celebrate your imperfections, saying, "Wow, am I
  ever human."

You can treat your frailties with kindness.

You can be gentle with yourself and others.

You could run away. Or you can see this as the work you need to do right now.

You could fight and rail against this. Or you can work with these circumstances to see what's possible here and now.

You could stay, thrashing in the sadness, the anger, the fear. Or you can stop. You can breathe.

You can praise who you are and all you do at least as often as you pick yourself apart.

You can practice the good thoughts, the hopeful thoughts.

You can think of your flaws as moxie practice.

You can see you differently.

Look at yourself with love and tenderness.

Hold what needs work, hold your vulnerability, your humanity with the greatest care. If it doesn't work, try again in five minutes. In an hour. Tomorrow.

Life is hard. Do your best. Love your self. *Love* your self. Remember, pretty flowers come from shit.

Encore yourself with joy, baby

Shakespeare said, "All the world's a stage."

And he's right.

We perform our roles, again and again.

Sometimes we like our roles, our performances.

Sometimes we don't.

But then there might come a day when the performance is over, when we no longer get to play that part.

We no longer get to be with that person.

And we can exit the stage, pack our bags, and literally or metaphorically climb aboard an old stinky bus and ride into the dark and soul-crushing night.

We can tear ourselves apart inside as we wonder, "What's next?"

God, that can suck.

Because all you know is what has been.

And who knows what will come.

And the more important the role was to you, the more important the person was to you, the harder this will be.

If that particular performance is over, if you no longer
  get to play that part or be with that person, if you are
  backstage, in the dark, wondering what's next,
  do not encore your sufferings.

Do not encore your failings.

Do not encore your regrets or shortcomings.

Do not do an encore full of fear and trembling.

When you are in the dark wondering what's next, dream
  bigly.

Open your mouth and your heart widely.

Encore yourself with attitude, joy, and confidence, baby.

You are fekkin' fierce.

Step back into the light.

Bring new work to a new stage.

Bold work.

That pushes the boundaries.

Work that pushes yourself.

Try new things.

And then hear the audience roar.

In this new space, see what is

Sit.

Settle.

Inhale.

Exhale.

Everything goes.

This breath.

This moment.

This life.

Everything goes.

Sit with this fact.

Be with this season when it comes, and when it demands
that everything goes.

Sit.

Still.

When you are asked to let go, when you have been
stripped down to the bone, if you have to, take some
time to feel defeated.

To surrender to the sorrow and pain.

Sit.

Breathe.

Inhale.

Exhale.

When you have been stripped down to the bone, can you
see that there is actually some spaciousness in that?

Then, can you hold onto that spaciousness, staying
curious, light, soft?

When the season of letting go comes, be alive at your
core.

When the season of letting go comes, resist clinging to
what should be.

Do not wallow in what has been.

Do not let yourself grow rotten with misery.

In this new space, see what is.

Let things happen.

In such a season, may you find quiet.

In such a season, may you find clarity.

In such a reckoning, may you surrender and ground.

A new season is on its way.

You deserve to be looked at with love and grace

Dear one, you are beautiful.

Hush.

Do not argue.

Do not gather all of your usual evidence to try and prove
to me how and why that is not the case.

Dear one, you are beautiful.

If you are among those who hear that message often
and from a multitude of voices, I am so very happy
for you.

If you are among those who have not heard that message
in a very long time, my heart holds you.

You. Are. Beautiful.

You are a most miraculous work.

You need to know that.

And if you are among those who do know that, praise be.

If you are among those who have forgotten that, here is a
voice, reaching through the wilderness to tell you—
you are beautiful. Miraculous.

Rare as a bird's nest made out of horse hair.

Dear one, you deserve to be looked at with love and grace.

You deserve to know you matter. You are worthy. You are
　　enough.

Inhale.

Exhale.

Breathe.

Center.

Dear one, never forget it. You. Are. Beautiful.

Part Six

What You've Done/Are Doing/ Will Do

What deserves your attention?

You are here.
You are grounded.
You are loved.
You are loving.
You are brave.
You are open.
You are alive.
You inhabit a body.
You have a beautiful form.
You can have a future of abundance.
You can put into place the things that will create a better
    future.
For yourself. For your family. For the world.
You can be full of wonder.
Sit.
Breathe.
You are quiet.
You are centered.
You know this—your thoughts affect your reality.

Be awed by the incredible person that you are.

Be amazed by the ant. And the butterfly.

Be grateful for the air in your lungs, the food in your belly.

From this space, ask, "What inner obstacles do I need to face?"

Breathe in.

Breathe out.

From this space, ask, "What do I need to release?"

Inhale.

Exhale.

From this space, ask, "What deserves my attention?"

It could be your body. Your spirit. It could be someone around you. Or the world.

Take a deep breath in.

Let the breath go.

You.

Take care of you.

Take care of those you love.

Be well.

Befriend your scars and your heart.

Grow spacious and alive.

Can you tell when you are growing prickly?

Come.
Sit.
Breathe.
Live.
In this moment.
In this space.
Inhale.
Exhale.
Do you ever feel prickly?
Everything annoys.
The sound of someone chewing.
How long the stoplight stays red.
The price of milk.
The crack in the sidewalk that trips you every single time.
Come.
Sit.
Breathe.
Live.
In this moment.

In this space.

Inhale.

Exhale.

Can you tell when you are growing prickly?

When you are going to take everything personally.

When you are going to say something you will regret.

When you are going to make the mindless choice.

Come.

Sit.

Breathe.

Live.

In this moment.

In this space.

Inhale.

Exhale.

Be.

Still.

Be.

Still.

And it might have been horrible, harrowing, but you have survived

Feel yourself settle.

Inhale.

Exhale.

In the Zen Buddhist tradition, they use "encouragement sticks" to bring disciples to awakening.

Inhale.

Exhale.

Now imagine a stick, whacking you in the back.

What. The. Hell.

But isn't that what life does sometimes?

Inhale.

Exhale.

Whack.

For me it was chemo and divorce.

Inhale.

Exhale.

What has it been for you?

Inhale.

Exhale.

What has smacked you upside the head?

Inhale.

Exhale.

What has demanded you find every last bit of strength and courage you have left?

Inhale.

Exhale.

But if you are reading this right now, you have survived.

Inhale.

Exhale.

And it might have been horrible, harrowing, but you have survived.

Inhale.

Exhale.

You are here. Now.

If you are facing the battle of your life, know that I am here, cheering you on.

Maybe it is a good time to surrender

Turn in.

Tune in to you.

Inhale.

Exhale.

When it gets bad, do you ever catch yourself asking, "What's the point? Why get up? Why try? What difference does it make? What difference do I make?"

Maybe life used to feel new. Lush. Full of possibility.

Maybe you used to feel alive.

Maybe you've wandered into a desert of the spirit. You are dry. And covered in things that hurt.

Are you tempted to put your hands up in surrender?

Maybe it *is* a good time to surrender.

To surrender all that has passed.

To surrender the stories holding you back and keeping you down.

But when it gets bad, do not give up.

You get to pick the way to handle this adventure you are on—whether it is one of your own choosing or not.

If you are lost in a desert of the spirit, you can choose to
keep going.

Try and find a friend to walk through the valley with you.

Make sure to find all the coolness you can along your path.

Rest.

Trust that you will walk out of this with a story to tell.

Or you can choose to be like a cactus in your desert.

Stand tall.

Stand still.

Wait.

Let the sun, stars, and scorpions come and go.

Inhale.

Exhale.

One day, a bird will brave the needles.

One day, a bird with wings and a song will burrow in
your living heart.

You are bigger than your thinks

You've probably done some shit.

I have too.

And, oh, how all the bad things you've done, all the ways you've fallen short, can weigh a person down.

It can be tempting to pull away, tempting to crawl into a dark hole, because you don't want to be a bother. Because who would want to listen or be with you, because who could understand, because who could ever love a person like you again?

Is that what your voices say?

We've all done some shit.

When that weighs on us, we need to remember, it's what makes us human.

When that weighs on us, we need to be honest about what we've done, but then we need to turn toward and repair instead of turn away and isolate.

Everything you've done is a chance for growth.

You deserve love.

Turn toward.

You deserve to be heard.

Reach out.

You deserve peace.

Be gentle with yourself.

You are bigger than your thinks.

Let me repeat that—you are bigger than your thinks.

You are more than what you've done.

You are moving the obstacles from the past out of the
way, so you can step freely and easily into the future.

You have already done so much

Have you ever felt hammered? And not the good kind?
But the kind where life feels like it's a sledgehammer and
you're the target getting whaled on?
Maybe the bad news won't stop.
Maybe it's one crisis in the midst of another, one loss
after another.
Maybe the demands are too much and your resources
too few.
Sit.
Breathe.
You are alive.
You are here.
You have done so much already.
Let me say that again.
You have done so much already.
You can rely on yourself.
You are strong. Strong enough to face this obstacle. And
the next.
You can feel defeated, and rightly so. Life can be so hard.
So very, very hard.

But you can also see this as a chance to become the best
version of yourself.

Because hammered can also mean to have worked
laboriously. To have put into shape with great effort.

Hammered can mean you have used your drive and will
to see the results you want to see.

When life hits, sit.

Breathe.

Settle—moment into moment.

You are alive.

You are here.

You are meant to be here.

Be grateful to the self you have been.

Love who you are becoming. A bad ass with a hammer,
working hard to shape the life you want.

You have a light inside

Feel your sitting bones ground.
That means quit living in your head.
Feel your sitting bones ground.
Now feel your breath grow deep.
The darkness always pretends it's forever.
It isn't.
Right now, it's like this.
This will pass.
Breathe.
Sit.
The darkness pretends it's forever, but it's not.
And anyways, you have a light inside.
Listen to me.
You have a light inside.
It might feel as small and distant as a star drowning in a
    cold sea of darkness, but it is there.
Sit.
Breathe.
See your light.

How can you feed it?

How can you help it grow?

Please, don't believe the sharp teeth inside.

Do not feed them your soft spirit.

Move quietly and gently away, step by step, inch by inch, until you are in a safe place.

A place where you can remind yourself.

Your spirit is fierce.

Relentless.

It is tied in with the stars.

And the roots of trees.

The darkness always pretends it's forever.

But what if you stop?

Pause. Breathe.

What if you meet the darkness the way a firefly does?

You are a bad ass. With your very own light. And your very own wings.

This is not the end of your story

When things get tough, be kind to yourself.

When things get challenging, name the things in your life that are going right.

When life keeps telling you no, look for the yes—big or small.

Yes, you can breathe.

Yes, you can rest.

Yes, you can smile.

Yes, you can endure.

When your thoughts threaten to take over your heart and mind, remind yourself that it's okay.

You are doing the best you can.

When your thoughts threaten to ruin your relationships, say, "Hey, I'm struggling."

When the darkness threatens, say, "It sucks pretty bad. But this is the path I'm on right now."

When you are tempted to pull out the clobber narrative and start berating yourself, think, "How would I talk to a friend who is going through this?"

The worse you feel, the kinder you need to be to yourself.

You can choose which thoughts you pick up.

Which thoughts you feed.

Even though you can't see all the details, even though you
don't know what direction they might take you in, trust
that there are many more narratives in your future.

This is not the end of your story.

Another chapter is already on its way.